RATIOS AND PROPORTIONAL RELATIONSHIPS

MATH BOOK GRADE 6
CHILDREN'S MATH BOOKS

BABY PROFESSOR
EDUCATION KIDS

Speedy Publishing LLC
40 E. Main St. #1156
Newark, DE 19711
www.speedypublishing.com
Copyright 2017

A proportion is an equation with a ratio on each side. It is a statement that two ratios are equal.

4/5 = 8/10 is an example of a proportion.

EXERCISE NO. 1

(1) $98 : 100 =$

(2) $24 : 72 =$

(3) $24 : 28 =$

(4) $24 : 86 =$

(5) $24 : 94 =$

(6) $24 : 75 =$

(7) $24 : 54 =$

(8) $24 : 88 =$

(9) $24 : 46 =$

(10) $95 : 100 =$

EXERCISE NO. 2

(1) $87 : 93 =$

(2) $87 : 99 =$

(3) $87 : 96 =$

(4) $44 : 86 =$

(5) $44 : 88 =$

(6) $87 : 90 =$

(7) $44 : 60 =$

(8) $44 : 96 =$

(9) $44 : 56 =$

(10) $44 : 66 =$

EXERCISE NO. 3

(1) $70 : 77 =$

(2) $70 : 86 =$

(3) $70 : 91 =$

(4) $70 : 85 =$

(5) $70 : 94 =$

(6) $70 : 84 =$

(7) $70 : 76 =$

(8) $70 : 98 =$

(9) $70 : 96 =$

(10) $70 : 82 =$

EXERCISE NO. 4

(1) $65 : 78 =$

(2) $39 : 45 =$

(3) $65 : 100 =$

(4) $65 : 85 =$

(5) $65 : 75 =$

(6) $65 : 90 =$

(7) $65 : 80 =$

(8) $65 : 91 =$

(9) $65 : 95 =$

(10) $65 : 70 =$

EXERCISE NO. 5

(1) $92 : 98 =$

(2) $92 : 96 =$

(3) $92 : 94 =$

(4) $40 : 88 =$

(5) $40 : 78 =$

(6) $40 : 62 =$

(7) $40 : 58 =$

(8) $92 : 100 =$

(9) $40 : 90 =$

(10) $40 : 80 =$

EXERCISE NO. 6

(1) 33 : 51 =

(2) 33 : 63 =

(3) 33 : 88 =

(4) 33 : 93 =

(5) 33 : 72 =

(6) 33 : 87 =

(7) 33 : 69 =

(8) 33 : 45 =

(9) 33 : 90 =

(10) 33 : 78 =

EXERCISE NO. 7

(1) 18 : 40 =

(2) 18 : 50 =

(3) 18 : 56 =

(4) 18 : 80 =

(5) 18 : 44 =

(6) 18 : 99 =

(7) 18 : 36 =

(8) 18 : 88 =

(9) 18 : 82 =

(10) 18 : 84 =

EXERCISE NO. 8

(1) $34 : 78 =$

(2) $34 : 52 =$

(3) $34 : 38 =$

(4) $34 : 58 =$

(5) $34 : 36 =$

(6) $34 : 100 =$

(7) $34 : 68 =$

(8) $34 : 94 =$

(9) $34 : 82 =$

(10) $34 : 60 =$

EXERCISE NO. 9

(1) 28 : 40 =

(2) 28 : 30 =

(3) 28 : 84 =

(4) 28 : 66 =

(5) 28 : 76 =

(6) 28 : 50 =

(7) 28 : 88 =

(8) 28 : 91 =

(9) 28 : 77 =

(10) 28 : 49 =

EXERCISE NO. 10

(1) $82 : 88 =$

(2) $82 : 84 =$

(3) $82 : 92 =$

(4) $82 : 94 =$

(5) $82 : 100 =$

(6) $82 : 86 =$

(7) $82 : 96 =$

(8) $82 : 90 =$

(9) $84 : 91 =$

(10) $82 : 98 =$

Find the equivalent ratio. Write the answer in each box.

EXERCISE NO. 11

(1) $5 : 16 \ = \ \boxed{} : 32 \ = \ 15 : \boxed{} \ = \ 20 : \boxed{} \ = \ 25 : \boxed{}$

(2) $3 : 8 \ = \ 6 : \boxed{} \ = \ 9 : \boxed{} \ = \ \boxed{} : 32 \ = \ 15 : \boxed{}$

(3) $1 : 2 \ = \ \boxed{} : 4 \ = \ \boxed{} : 6 \ = \ 4 : \boxed{} \ = \ 5 : \boxed{}$

(4) $3 : 10 \ = \ 6 : \boxed{} \ = \ 9 : \boxed{} \ = \ 12 : \boxed{} \ = \ 15 : \boxed{}$

(5) $5 : 14 \ = \ \boxed{} : 28 \ = \ 15 : \boxed{} \ = \ 20 : \boxed{} \ = \ 25 : \boxed{}$

(6) $3 : 5 \ = \ 6 : \boxed{} \ = \ 9 : \boxed{} \ = \ 12 : \boxed{} \ = \ \boxed{} : 25$

(7) $5 : 9 \ = \ \boxed{} : 18 \ = \ \boxed{} : 27 \ = \ \boxed{} : 36 \ = \ \boxed{} : 45$

(8) $5 : 6 \ = \ 10 : \boxed{} \ = \ \boxed{} : 18 \ = \ 20 : \boxed{} \ = \ \boxed{} : 30$

EXERCISE NO. 12

(1) $13 : 19 \ = \ 26 : \square \ = \ \square : 57 \ = \ \square : 76 \ = \ \square : 95$

(2) $13 : 25 \ = \ 26 : \square \ = \ 39 : \square \ = \ 52 : \square \ = \ 65 : \square$

(3) $13 : 22 \ = \ \square : 44 \ = \ 39 : \square \ = \ \square : 88 \ = \ 65 : \square$

(4) $13 : 18 \ = \ 26 : \square \ = \ 39 : \square \ = \ 52 : \square \ = \ \square : 90$

(5) $13 : 20 \ = \ \square : 40 \ = \ 39 : \square \ = \ \square : 80 \ = \ 65 : \square$

(6) $2 : 3 \ = \ 4 : \square \ = \ \square : 9 \ = \ \square : 12 \ = \ 10 : \square$

(7) $13 : 17 \ = \ 26 : \square \ = \ \square : 51 \ = \ 52 : \square \ = \ \square : 85$

(8) $13 : 21 \ = \ 26 : \square \ = \ 39 : \square \ = \ 52 : \square \ = \ \square : 105$

EXERCISE NO. 13

(1) $13 : 14 \ = \ \boxed{} : 28 \ = \ 39 : \boxed{} \ = \ 52 : \boxed{} \ = \ 65 : \boxed{}$

(2) $1 : 3 \ = \ \boxed{} : 6 \ = \ 3 : \boxed{} \ = \ 4 : \boxed{} \ = \ 5 : \boxed{}$

(3) $13 : 17 \ = \ 26 : \boxed{} \ = \ 39 : \boxed{} \ = \ \boxed{} : 68 \ = \ \boxed{} : 85$

(4) $13 : 23 \ = \ \boxed{} : 46 \ = \ 39 : \boxed{} \ = \ 52 : \boxed{} \ = \ \boxed{} : 115$

(5) $2 : 3 \ = \ 4 : \boxed{} \ = \ \boxed{} : 9 \ = \ \boxed{} : 12 \ = \ 10 : \boxed{}$

(6) $13 : 21 \ = \ 26 : \boxed{} \ = \ \boxed{} : 63 \ = \ 52 : \boxed{} \ = \ \boxed{} : 105$

(7) $1 : 2 \ = \ 2 : \boxed{} \ = \ \boxed{} : 6 \ = \ \boxed{} : 8 \ = \ 5 : \boxed{}$

(8) $1 : 4 \ = \ 2 : \boxed{} \ = \ \boxed{} : 12 \ = \ 4 : \boxed{} \ = \ \boxed{} : 20$

EXERCISE NO. 14

(1) $2 : 5 \ = \ \boxed{} : 10 \ = \ 6 : \boxed{} \ = \ \boxed{} : 20 \ = \ 10 : \boxed{}$

(2) $2 : 3 \ = \ 4 : \boxed{} \ = \ 6 : \boxed{} \ = \ 8 : \boxed{} \ = \ 10 : \boxed{}$

(3) $9 : 11 \ = \ \boxed{} : 22 \ = \ 27 : \boxed{} \ = \ \boxed{} : 44 \ = \ \boxed{} : 55$

(4) $6 : 11 \ = \ \boxed{} : 22 \ = \ \boxed{} : 33 \ = \ \boxed{} : 44 \ = \ \boxed{} : 55$

(5) $9 : 22 \ = \ \boxed{} : 44 \ = \ 27 : \boxed{} \ = \ 36 : \boxed{} \ = \ \boxed{} : 110$

(6) $9 : 25 \ = \ 18 : \boxed{} \ = \ \boxed{} : 75 \ = \ \boxed{} : 100 \ = \ \boxed{} : 125$

(7) $6 : 7 \ = \ 12 : \boxed{} \ = \ 18 : \boxed{} \ = \ 24 : \boxed{} \ = \ 30 : \boxed{}$

(8) $3 : 8 \ = \ 6 : \boxed{} \ = \ 9 : \boxed{} \ = \ 12 : \boxed{} \ = \ 15 : \boxed{}$

EXERCISE NO. 15

(1) $3 : 13 \;=\; 6 : \square \;=\; 9 : \square \;=\; 12 : \square \;=\; 15 : \square$

(2) $1 : 2 \;=\; 2 : \square \;=\; 3 : \square \;=\; 4 : \square \;=\; 5 : \square$

(3) $3 : 7 \;=\; 6 : \square \;=\; \square : 21 \;=\; 12 : \square \;=\; 15 : \square$

(4) $3 : 5 \;=\; \square : 10 \;=\; \square : 15 \;=\; 12 : \square \;=\; 15 : \square$

(5) $3 : 4 \;=\; 6 : \square \;=\; 9 : \square \;=\; 12 : \square \;=\; \square : 20$

(6) $3 : 10 \;=\; 6 : \square \;=\; \square : 30 \;=\; \square : 40 \;=\; 15 : \square$

(7) $3 : 11 \;=\; \square : 22 \;=\; 9 : \square \;=\; \square : 44 \;=\; 15 : \square$

(8) $3 : 8 \;=\; \square : 16 \;=\; \square : 24 \;=\; \square : 32 \;=\; 15 : \square$

EXERCISE NO. 16

(1) $5 : 18 \quad = \quad \square : 36 \quad = \quad 15 : \square \quad = \quad \square : 72 \quad = \quad \square : 90$

(2) $5 : 12 \quad = \quad \square : 24 \quad = \quad \square : 36 \quad = \quad \square : 48 \quad = \quad \square : 60$

(3) $2 : 7 \quad = \quad 4 : \square \quad = \quad 6 : \square \quad = \quad 8 : \square \quad = \quad \square : 35$

(4) $5 : 8 \quad = \quad \square : 16 \quad = \quad 15 : \square \quad = \quad 20 : \square \quad = \quad \square : 40$

(5) $1 : 4 \quad = \quad \square : 8 \quad = \quad \square : 12 \quad = \quad 4 : \square \quad = \quad 5 : \square$

(6) $5 : 9 \quad = \quad 10 : \square \quad = \quad 15 : \square \quad = \quad 20 : \square \quad = \quad 25 : \square$

(7) $5 : 17 \quad = \quad 10 : \square \quad = \quad 15 : \square \quad = \quad 20 : \square \quad = \quad 25 : \square$

(8) $1 : 3 \quad = \quad \square : 6 \quad = \quad 3 : \square \quad = \quad \square : 12 \quad = \quad 5 : \square$

EXERCISE NO. 17

(1) $13 : 19 \ = \ \boxed{} : 38 \ = \ 39 : \boxed{} \ = \ \boxed{} : 76 \ = \ \boxed{} : 95$

(2) $13 : 20 \ = \ \boxed{} : 40 \ = \ 39 : \boxed{} \ = \ 52 : \boxed{} \ = \ 65 : \boxed{}$

(3) $13 : 14 \ = \ 26 : \boxed{} \ = \ 39 : \boxed{} \ = \ \boxed{} : 56 \ = \ \boxed{} : 70$

(4) $13 : 17 \ = \ \boxed{} : 34 \ = \ \boxed{} : 51 \ = \ \boxed{} : 68 \ = \ 65 : \boxed{}$

(5) $2 : 3 \ = \ \boxed{} : 6 \ = \ \boxed{} : 9 \ = \ \boxed{} : 12 \ = \ 10 : \boxed{}$

(6) $13 : 15 \ = \ 26 : \boxed{} \ = \ \boxed{} : 45 \ = \ 52 : \boxed{} \ = \ 65 : \boxed{}$

(7) $13 : 16 \ = \ 26 : \boxed{} \ = \ \boxed{} : 48 \ = \ \boxed{} : 64 \ = \ \boxed{} : 80$

(8) $1 : 2 \ = \ \boxed{} : 4 \ = \ \boxed{} : 6 \ = \ \boxed{} : 8 \ = \ \boxed{} : 10$

EXERCISE NO. 18

(1) $11 : 15 \quad = \quad 22 : \square \quad = \quad \square : 45 \quad = \quad \square : 60 \quad = \quad \square : 75$

(2) $5 : 11 \quad = \quad \square : 22 \quad = \quad \square : 33 \quad = \quad 20 : \square \quad = \quad 25 : \square$

(3) $11 : 14 \quad = \quad \square : 28 \quad = \quad \square : 42 \quad = \quad \square : 56 \quad = \quad 55 : \square$

(4) $5 : 6 \quad = \quad \square : 12 \quad = \quad 15 : \square \quad = \quad \square : 24 \quad = \quad 25 : \square$

(5) $11 : 12 \quad = \quad \square : 24 \quad = \quad \square : 36 \quad = \quad \square : 48 \quad = \quad 55 : \square$

(6) $5 : 13 \quad = \quad 10 : \square \quad = \quad \square : 39 \quad = \quad 20 : \square \quad = \quad 25 : \square$

(7) $11 : 13 \quad = \quad 22 : \square \quad = \quad \square : 39 \quad = \quad \square : 52 \quad = \quad \square : 65$

(8) $1 : 2 \quad = \quad 2 : \square \quad = \quad \square : 6 \quad = \quad \square : 8 \quad = \quad 5 : \square$

EXERCISE NO. 19

(1) $2 : 3 \; = \; 4 : \square \; = \; 6 : \square \; = \; \square : 12 \; = \; 10 : \square$

(2) $1 : 2 \; = \; \square : 4 \; = \; 3 : \square \; = \; 4 : \square \; = \; 5 : \square$

(3) $5 : 11 \; = \; \square : 22 \; = \; \square : 33 \; = \; \square : 44 \; = \; \square : 55$

(4) $5 : 6 \; = \; 10 : \square \; = \; \square : 18 \; = \; \square : 24 \; = \; \square : 30$

(5) $5 : 12 \; = \; 10 : \square \; = \; \square : 36 \; = \; \square : 48 \; = \; 25 : \square$

(6) $5 : 13 \; = \; 10 : \square \; = \; \square : 39 \; = \; 20 : \square \; = \; 25 : \square$

(7) $2 : 5 \; = \; 4 : \square \; = \; 6 : \square \; = \; 8 : \square \; = \; 10 : \square$

(8) $5 : 8 \; = \; 10 : \square \; = \; 15 : \square \; = \; 20 : \square \; = \; 25 : \square$

EXERCISE NO. 20

(1) $15 : 16 \ = \ \square : 32 \ = \ 45 : \square \ = \ 60 : \square \ = \ 75 : \square$

(2) $9 : 10 \ = \ 18 : \square \ = \ 27 : \square \ = \ \square : 40 \ = \ 45 : \square$

(3) $13 : 17 \ = \ \square : 34 \ = \ \square : 51 \ = \ \square : 68 \ = \ \square : 85$

(4) $5 : 6 \ = \ \square : 12 \ = \ \square : 18 \ = \ 20 : \square \ = \ 25 : \square$

(5) $9 : 11 \ = \ 18 : \square \ = \ 27 : \square \ = \ \square : 44 \ = \ 45 : \square$

(6) $15 : 19 \ = \ \square : 38 \ = \ 45 : \square \ = \ 60 : \square \ = \ \square : 95$

(7) $3 : 4 \ = \ \square : 8 \ = \ 9 : \square \ = \ 12 : \square \ = \ 15 : \square$

(8) $15 : 17 \ = \ \square : 34 \ = \ \square : 51 \ = \ \square : 68 \ = \ 75 : \square$

EXERCISE NO. 21

1) Which two teachers received equivalent ratios of apples from their total number of students? _____

Teachers	Received Apples	Number of Students
Brown	2	34
Hearn	3	51
Theodore	2	36
Jones	3	48

2) Which two types of cars have equivalent ratios of miles traveled to gallons of gas used? _____

Cars	Miles Traveled	Gallons of Gas Used
Chevrolet	27	3
Toyota	64	4
Ford	25	2
Dodge	48	3

3) Which two recipes have equivalent ratios of cups of flour needed to the number of cookies? _____

Recipes	Cups of Flour Needed	Number of Cookies
Sugar	4	32
Macadamia Nut	5	40
Chocolate Chip	4	34
Peanut Butter	2	17

EXERCISE NO. 22

1) Which two baseball games have equivalent ratios of walks to the number of runs scored? _____

Games	Walks	Number of Runs Scored
Yankees	2	17
Braves	5	40
Red Sox	4	32
Cubs	4	34

2) Which two types of cars have equivalent ratios of miles traveled to gallons of gas used? _____

Cars	Miles Traveled	Gallons of Gas Used
Fiat	46	3
Ford	42	3
Toyota	48	4
Lexus	28	2

3) Which two recycling plants have equivalent ratios of green bottles to the total number of bottles recycled in one day? _____

Recycling Plants	Green Bottles Recycled	Total Bottles Recycled
Plant A	23	115
Plant B	48	216
Plant C	50	260
Plant D	64	320

EXERCISE NO. 23

1) Which two types of cars have equivalent ratios of miles traveled to gallons of gas used? _____

Cars	Miles Traveled	Gallons of Gas Used
Chevrolet	22	2
Toyota	40	4
Fiat	33	3
Ford	32	3

2) Which two recycling plants have equivalent ratios of green bottles to the total number of bottles recycled in one day? _____

Recycling Plants	Green Bottles Recycled	Total Bottles Recycled
Plant A	13	104
Plant B	18	140
Plant C	32	256
Plant D	24	196

3) Which two city parks have equivalent ratios of planted maple trees to the total number of trees in the park? _____

City Parks	Maple Trees Planted	Total Trees Planted
South Side	24	158
Eastern	42	294
Central	17	119
North Ridge	36	248

EXERCISE NO. 24

1) Which two types of cars have equivalent ratios of miles traveled to hours of time during the trip? _____

Cars	Miles Traveled	Hours of Time
Chevrolet	34	2
Toyota	51	3
Lexus	36	2
Honda	48	3

2) Which two teachers received equivalent ratios of apples from their total number of students? _____

Teachers	Received Apples	Number of Students
Jones	3	46
Theodore	3	42
Brown	2	28
Smith	4	48

3) Which two recipes have equivalent ratios of cups of flour needed to the number of cookies? _____

Recipes	Cups of Flour Needed	Number of Cookies
Chocolate Chip	3	48
Macadamia Nut	2	25
Peanut Butter	4	64
Oatmeal Raisin	3	27

EXERCISE NO. 25

1) Which two recipes have equivalent ratios of cups of flour needed to the number of cookies? _____

Recipes	Cups of Flour Needed	Number of Cookies
Oatmeal Raisin	2	17
Sugar	4	32
Macadamia Nut	4	34
Peanut Butter	5	40

2) Which two types of cars have equivalent ratios of miles traveled to gallons of gas used? _____

Cars	Miles Traveled	Gallons of Gas Used
Toyota	25	2
Ford	64	4
Fiat	48	3
Dodge	27	3

3) Which two baseball games have equivalent ratios of walks to the number of runs scored? _____

Games	Walks	Number of Runs Scored
Braves	1	14
Yankees	2	32
Marlins	2	24
Red Sox	3	36

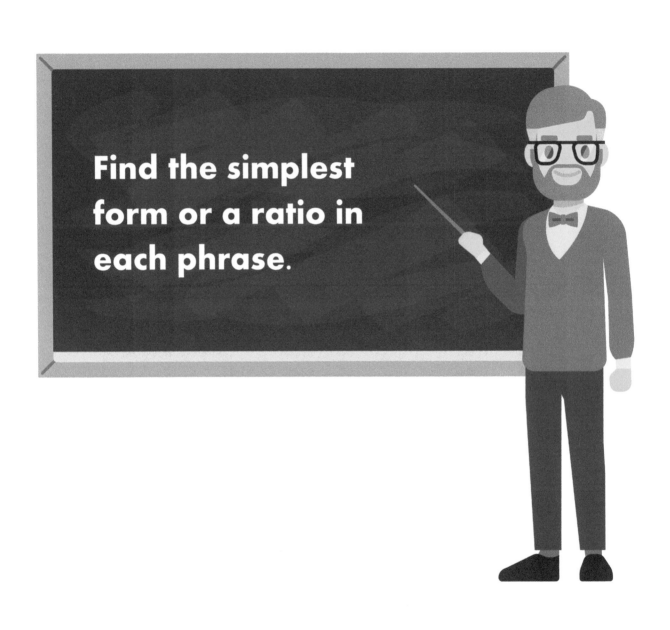

Find the simplest form or a ratio in each phrase.

EXERCISE NO. 26

1) 2 red bikes out of 24 bikes _____

2) 5 inches to 25 inches _____

3) 32 footballs to 48 footballs _____

4) 8 snow days out of 332 days _____

5) 6 blue cars out of 21 cars _____

6) 12 points out of 24 points _____

7) 6 feet out of 42 feet _____

8) 6 cups to 48 cups _____

9) 18 gallons to 33 gallons _____

10) 40 pounds to 50 pounds _____

11) 8 beetles out of 20 insects _____

12) 14 pints to 21 pints _____

13) 33 miles out of 36 miles _____

14) 4 quarts to 12 quarts _____

15) 7 nickels to 70 nickels _____

16) 49 rainy days out of 56 days _____

17) 8 dimes out of 20 coins _____

18) 28 dimes to 49 dimes _____

EXERCISE NO. 27

1) 28 points out of 40 points _____

2) 15 footballs to 18 footballs _____

3) 5 nickels to 25 nickels _____

4) 12 dimes to 72 dimes _____

5) 20 snow days out of 45 days _____

6) 7 pounds to 28 pounds _____

7) 4 dimes out of 14 coins _____

8) 20 feet out of 48 feet _____

9) 40 beetles out of 55 insects _____

10) 12 cups to 21 cups _____

11) 10 cakes out of 18 cakes _____

12) 18 miles out of 36 miles _____

13) 7 inches to 49 inches _____

14) 22 quarts to 24 quarts _____

15) 2 pennies to 24 pennies _____

16) 24 rainy days out of 48 days _____

17) 12 pints to 66 pints _____

18) 42 red bikes out of 49 bikes _____

EXERCISE NO. 28

1) 10 pennies to 35 pennies _____

2) 24 inches to 27 inches _____

3) 24 cups to 40 cups _____

4) 12 red bikes out of 30 bikes _____

5) 48 quarts to 60 quarts _____

6) 35 miles out of 55 miles _____

7) 42 snow days out of 54 days _____

8) 14 blue cars out of 84 cars _____

9) 15 rainy days out of 33 days _____

10) 2 dimes out of 6 coins _____

11) 4 feet out of 6 feet _____

12) 30 nickels to 55 nickels _____

13) 20 gallons to 25 gallons _____

14) 42 points out of 56 points _____

15) 4 pounds to 44 pounds _____

16) 12 beetles out of 14 insects _____

17) 9 footballs to 30 footballs _____

18) 36 cakes out of 54 cakes _____

EXERCISE NO. 29

1) 10 gallons to 50 gallons _____

2) 25 cups to 45 cups _____

3) 8 footballs to 48 footballs _____

4) 48 dimes to 66 dimes _____

5) 9 beetles out of 30 insects _____

6) 14 miles out of 77 miles _____

7) 30 snow days out of 72 days _____

8) 12 feet out of 48 feet _____

9) 6 rainy days out of 72 days _____

10) 25 quarts to 55 quarts _____

11) 7 pints to 77 pints _____

12) 24 pounds to 30 pounds _____

13) 20 nickels to 24 nickels _____

14) 6 pennies to 249 pennies _____

15) 10 inches to 14 inches _____

16) 30 points out of 48 points _____

17) 35 cakes out of 42 cakes _____

18) 30 blue cars out of 35 cars _____

EXERCISE NO. 30

1) 12 feet out of 24 feet _____

2) 12 dimes to 40 dimes _____

3) 8 gallons to 16 gallons _____

4) 49 quarts to 63 quarts _____

5) 3 cakes out of 21 cakes _____

6) 18 nickels to 20 nickels _____

7) 48 inches to 66 inches _____

8) 6 blue cars out of 24 cars _____

9) 35 miles out of 56 miles _____

10) 20 snow days out of 35 days _____

11) 66 pints to 72 pints _____

12) 49 rainy days out of 56 days _____

13) 20 points out of 45 points _____

14) 56 pounds to 70 pounds _____

15) 6 footballs to 27 footballs _____

16) 12 red bikes out of 28 bikes _____

17) 14 pennies to 77 pennies _____

18) 20 cups to 55 cups _____

Complete the equivalent proportions.

EXERCISE NO. 31

(1) $\dfrac{3}{88} = \dfrac{93}{x}$

(2) $\dfrac{100}{x} = \dfrac{25}{24}$

(3) $\dfrac{x}{84} = \dfrac{73}{4}$

(4) $\dfrac{3}{16} = \dfrac{15}{x}$

(5) $\dfrac{20}{9} = \dfrac{80}{x}$

(6) $\dfrac{20}{69} = \dfrac{40}{x}$

(7) $\dfrac{49}{6} = \dfrac{x}{18}$

(8) $\dfrac{9}{28} = \dfrac{45}{x}$

(9) $\dfrac{7}{17} = \dfrac{x}{68}$

(10) $\dfrac{x}{68} = \dfrac{40}{17}$

EXERCISE NO. 32

(1) $\dfrac{59}{4} = \dfrac{x}{52}$

(2) $\dfrac{x}{75} = \dfrac{67}{15}$

(3) $\dfrac{66}{x} = \dfrac{2}{51}$

(4) $\dfrac{x}{36} = \dfrac{13}{6}$

(5) $\dfrac{3}{74} = \dfrac{9}{x}$

(6) $\dfrac{7}{15} = \dfrac{28}{x}$

(7) $\dfrac{7}{65} = \dfrac{14}{x}$

(8) $\dfrac{97}{11} = \dfrac{x}{22}$

(9) $\dfrac{24}{67} = \dfrac{96}{x}$

(10) $\dfrac{91}{x} = \dfrac{13}{50}$

EXERCISE NO. 33

(1) $\dfrac{x}{45} = \dfrac{53}{15}$

(2) $\dfrac{x}{51} = \dfrac{65}{17}$

(3) $\dfrac{16}{x} = \dfrac{2}{3}$

(4) $\dfrac{11}{69} = \dfrac{44}{x}$

(5) $\dfrac{70}{x} = \dfrac{5}{47}$

(6) $\dfrac{45}{x} = \dfrac{3}{67}$

(7) $\dfrac{13}{9} = \dfrac{x}{36}$

(8) $\dfrac{7}{23} = \dfrac{49}{x}$

(9) $\dfrac{7}{47} = \dfrac{14}{x}$

(10) $\dfrac{x}{68} = \dfrac{57}{4}$

EXERCISE NO. 34

(1) $\dfrac{60}{x} = \dfrac{12}{65}$

(2) $\dfrac{44}{73} = \dfrac{88}{x}$

(3) $\dfrac{87}{23} = \dfrac{x}{46}$

(4) $\dfrac{5}{72} = \dfrac{10}{x}$

(5) $\dfrac{56}{27} = \dfrac{x}{81}$

(6) $\dfrac{13}{100} = \dfrac{52}{x}$

(7) $\dfrac{15}{37} = \dfrac{x}{74}$

(8) $\dfrac{12}{67} = \dfrac{24}{x}$

(9) $\dfrac{x}{36} = \dfrac{15}{2}$

(10) $\dfrac{x}{90} = \dfrac{85}{6}$

EXERCISE NO. 35

(1) $\dfrac{19}{53} = \dfrac{95}{x}$

(2) $\dfrac{4}{93} = \dfrac{60}{x}$

(3) $\dfrac{21}{x} = \dfrac{7}{88}$

(4) $\dfrac{69}{34} = \dfrac{x}{68}$

(5) $\dfrac{98}{x} = \dfrac{14}{79}$

(6) $\dfrac{24}{x} = \dfrac{6}{23}$

(7) $\dfrac{5}{27} = \dfrac{x}{81}$

(8) $\dfrac{x}{36} = \dfrac{63}{2}$

(9) $\dfrac{3}{13} = \dfrac{39}{x}$

(10) $\dfrac{88}{19} = \dfrac{x}{38}$

EXERCISE NO. 36

(1) $\dfrac{11}{29} = \dfrac{x}{58}$

(2) $\dfrac{11}{65} = \dfrac{33}{x}$

(3) $\dfrac{26}{7} = \dfrac{x}{49}$

(4) $\dfrac{81}{16} = \dfrac{x}{32}$

(5) $\dfrac{92}{5} = \dfrac{x}{35}$

(6) $\dfrac{x}{80} = \dfrac{29}{2}$

(7) $\dfrac{31}{9} = \dfrac{x}{54}$

(8) $\dfrac{11}{24} = \dfrac{44}{x}$

(9) $\dfrac{77}{x} = \dfrac{11}{6}$

(10) $\dfrac{2}{55} = \dfrac{86}{x}$

EXERCISE NO. 37

(1) $\dfrac{3}{46} = \dfrac{30}{x}$

(2) $\dfrac{7}{20} = \dfrac{56}{x}$

(3) $\dfrac{x}{78} = \dfrac{35}{2}$

(4) $\dfrac{x}{35} = \dfrac{97}{7}$

(5) $\dfrac{x}{95} = \dfrac{67}{19}$

(6) $\dfrac{32}{x} = \dfrac{2}{95}$

(7) $\dfrac{93}{11} = \dfrac{x}{44}$

(8) $\dfrac{27}{2} = \dfrac{x}{8}$

(9) $\dfrac{x}{66} = \dfrac{71}{11}$

(10) $\dfrac{x}{18} = \dfrac{71}{2}$

EXERCISE NO. 38

(1) $\dfrac{3}{26} = \dfrac{42}{x}$

(2) $\dfrac{5}{3} = \dfrac{80}{x}$

(3) $\dfrac{19}{11} = \dfrac{x}{99}$

(4) $\dfrac{39}{x} = \dfrac{3}{88}$

(5) $\dfrac{59}{6} = \dfrac{x}{18}$

(6) $\dfrac{3}{4} = \dfrac{x}{16}$

(7) $\dfrac{x}{72} = \dfrac{83}{4}$

(8) $\dfrac{62}{x} = \dfrac{31}{16}$

(9) $\dfrac{4}{7} = \dfrac{16}{x}$

(10) $\dfrac{34}{23} = \dfrac{x}{69}$

EXERCISE NO. 39

(1) $\dfrac{x}{68} = \dfrac{14}{17}$

(2) $\dfrac{23}{34} = \dfrac{92}{x}$

(3) $\dfrac{68}{x} = \dfrac{4}{87}$

(4) $\dfrac{x}{51} = \dfrac{46}{3}$

(5) $\dfrac{x}{63} = \dfrac{20}{7}$

(6) $\dfrac{3}{59} = \dfrac{96}{x}$

(7) $\dfrac{10}{51} = \dfrac{60}{x}$

(8) $\dfrac{x}{40} = \dfrac{47}{2}$

(9) $\dfrac{x}{48} = \dfrac{9}{4}$

(10) $\dfrac{28}{85} = \dfrac{56}{x}$

EXERCISE NO. 40

(1) $\dfrac{x}{48} = \dfrac{19}{3}$

(2) $\dfrac{74}{19} = \dfrac{x}{38}$

(3) $\dfrac{9}{2} = \dfrac{x}{70}$

(4) $\dfrac{42}{11} = \dfrac{84}{x}$

(5) $\dfrac{57}{10} = \dfrac{x}{30}$

(6) $\dfrac{84}{x} = \dfrac{14}{27}$

(7) $\dfrac{25}{19} = \dfrac{75}{x}$

(8) $\dfrac{3}{76} = \dfrac{57}{x}$

(9) $\dfrac{95}{x} = \dfrac{5}{74}$

(10) $\dfrac{7}{90} = \dfrac{63}{x}$

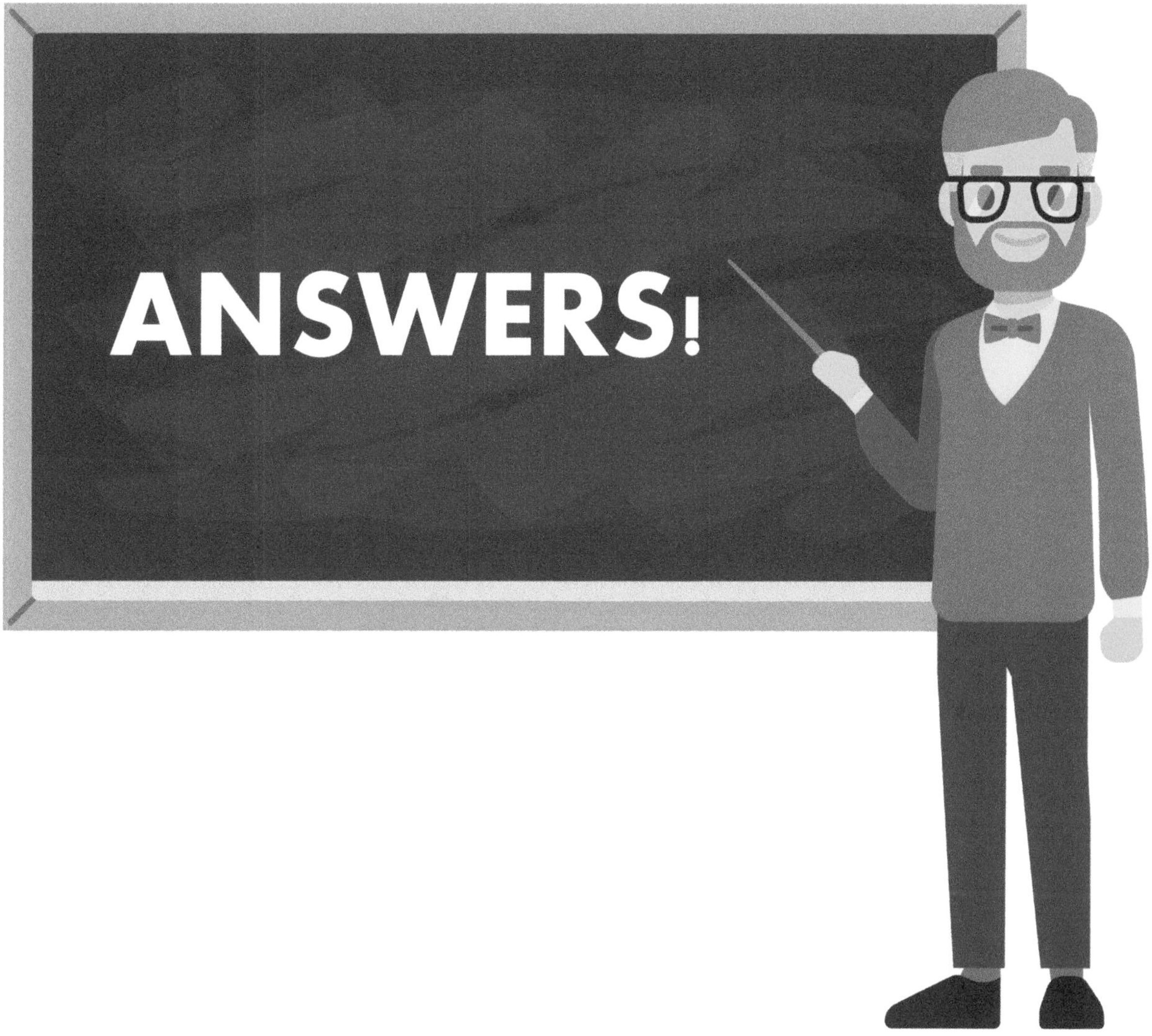
ANSWERS!

EXERCISE NO. 1

(1) 98 : 100 = $\boxed{49}$: 50

(2) 24 : 72 = $\boxed{1}$: 3

(3) 24 : 28 = $\boxed{6}$: 7

(4) 24 : 86 = $\boxed{12}$: 43

(5) 24 : 94 = $\boxed{12}$: 47

(6) 24 : 75 = $\boxed{8}$: 25

(7) 24 : 54 = $\boxed{4}$: 9

(8) 24 : 88 = $\boxed{3}$: 11

(9) 24 : 46 = $\boxed{12}$: 23

(10) 95 : 100 = $\boxed{19}$: 20

EXERCISE NO. 2

(1) 87 : 93 = $\boxed{29}$: 31

(2) 87 : 99 = $\boxed{29}$: 33

(3) 87 : 96 = $\boxed{29}$: 32

(4) 44 : 86 = $\boxed{22}$: 43

(5) 44 : 88 = $\boxed{1}$: 2

(6) 87 : 90 = $\boxed{29}$: 30

(7) 44 : 60 = $\boxed{11}$: 15

(8) 44 : 96 = $\boxed{11}$: 24

(9) 44 : 56 = $\boxed{11}$: 14

(10) 44 : 66 = $\boxed{2}$: 3

EXERCISE NO. 3

(1) 70 : 77 = $\boxed{10}$: 11

(2) 70 : 86 = $\boxed{35}$: 43

(3) 70 : 91 = $\boxed{10}$: 13

(4) 70 : 85 = $\boxed{14}$: 17

(5) 70 : 94 = $\boxed{35}$: 47

(6) 70 : 84 = $\boxed{5}$: 6

(7) 70 : 76 = $\boxed{35}$: 38

(8) 70 : 98 = $\boxed{5}$: 7

(9) 70 : 96 = $\boxed{35}$: 48

(10) 70 : 82 = $\boxed{35}$: 41

EXERCISE NO. 4

(1) 65 : 78 = $\boxed{5}$: 6

(2) 39 : 45 = $\boxed{13}$: 15

(3) 65 : 100 = $\boxed{13}$: 20

(4) 65 : 85 = $\boxed{13}$: 17

(5) 65 : 75 = $\boxed{13}$: 15

(6) 65 : 90 = $\boxed{13}$: 18

(7) 65 : 80 = $\boxed{13}$: 16

(8) 65 : 91 = $\boxed{5}$: 7

(9) 65 : 95 = $\boxed{13}$: 19

(10) 65 : 70 = $\boxed{13}$: 14

EXERCISE NO. 5

(1) $92 : 98 = \boxed{46} : 49$

(2) $92 : 96 = \boxed{23} : 24$

(3) $92 : 94 = \boxed{46} : 47$

(4) $40 : 88 = \boxed{5} : 11$

(5) $40 : 78 = \boxed{20} : 39$

(6) $40 : 62 = \boxed{20} : 31$

(7) $40 : 58 = \boxed{20} : 29$

(8) $92 : 100 = \boxed{23} : 25$

(9) $40 : 90 = \boxed{4} : 9$

(10) $40 : 80 = \boxed{1} : 2$

EXERCISE NO. 6

(1) $33 : 51 = \boxed{11} : 17$

(2) $33 : 63 = \boxed{11} : 21$

(3) $33 : 88 = \boxed{3} : 8$

(4) $33 : 93 = \boxed{11} : 31$

(5) $33 : 72 = \boxed{11} : 24$

(6) $33 : 87 = \boxed{11} : 29$

(7) $33 : 69 = \boxed{11} : 23$

(8) $33 : 45 = \boxed{11} : 15$

(9) $33 : 90 = \boxed{11} : 30$

(10) $33 : 78 = \boxed{11} : 26$

EXERCISE NO. 7

(1) $18 : 40 = \boxed{9} : 20$

(2) $18 : 50 = \boxed{9} : 25$

(3) $18 : 56 = \boxed{9} : 28$

(4) $18 : 80 = \boxed{9} : 40$

(5) $18 : 44 = \boxed{9} : 22$

(6) $18 : 99 = \boxed{2} : 11$

(7) $18 : 36 = \boxed{1} : 2$

(8) $18 : 88 = \boxed{9} : 44$

(9) $18 : 82 = \boxed{9} : 41$

(10) $18 : 84 = \boxed{3} : 14$

EXERCISE NO. 8

(1) $34 : 78 = \boxed{17} : 39$

(2) $34 : 52 = \boxed{17} : 26$

(3) $34 : 38 = \boxed{17} : 19$

(4) $34 : 58 = \boxed{17} : 29$

(5) $34 : 36 = \boxed{17} : 18$

(6) $34 : 100 = \boxed{17} : 50$

(7) $34 : 68 = \boxed{1} : 2$

(8) $34 : 94 = \boxed{17} : 47$

(9) $34 : 82 = \boxed{17} : 41$

(10) $34 : 60 = \boxed{17} : 30$

EXERCISE NO. 9

(1) 28 : 40 = 7 : 10

(2) 28 : 30 = 14 : 15

(3) 28 : 84 = 1 : 3

(4) 28 : 66 = 14 : 33

(5) 28 : 76 = 7 : 19

(6) 28 : 50 = 14 : 25

(7) 28 : 88 = 7 : 22

(8) 28 : 91 = 4 : 13

(9) 28 : 77 = 4 : 11

(10) 28 : 49 = 4 : 7

EXERCISE NO. 10

(1) 82 : 88 = 41 : 44

(2) 82 : 84 = 41 : 42

(3) 82 : 92 = 41 : 46

(4) 82 : 94 = 41 : 47

(5) 82 : 100 = 41 : 50

(6) 82 : 86 = 41 : 43

(7) 82 : 96 = 41 : 48

(8) 82 : 90 = 41 : 45

(9) 84 : 91 = 12 : 13

(10) 82 : 98 = 41 : 49

EXERCISE NO. 11

(1) 5 : 16 = 10 : 32 = 15 : 48 = 20 : 64 = 25 : 80

(2) 3 : 8 = 6 : 16 = 9 : 24 = 12 : 32 = 15 : 40

(3) 1 : 2 = 2 : 4 = 3 : 6 = 4 : 8 = 5 : 10

(4) 3 : 10 = 6 : 20 = 9 : 30 = 12 : 40 = 15 : 50

(5) 5 : 14 = 10 : 28 = 15 : 42 = 20 : 56 = 25 : 70

(6) 3 : 5 = 6 : 10 = 9 : 15 = 12 : 20 = 15 : 25

(7) 5 : 9 = 10 : 18 = 15 : 27 = 20 : 36 = 25 : 45

(8) 5 : 6 = 10 : 12 = 15 : 18 = 20 : 24 = 25 : 30

EXERCISE NO. 12

(1) 13 : 19 = 26 : 38 = 39 : 57 = 52 : 76 = 65 : 95

(2) 13 : 25 = 26 : 50 = 39 : 75 = 52 : 100 = 65 : 125

(3) 13 : 22 = 26 : 44 = 39 : 66 = 52 : 88 = 65 : 110

(4) 13 : 18 = 26 : 36 = 39 : 54 = 52 : 72 = 65 : 90

(5) 13 : 20 = 26 : 40 = 39 : 60 = 52 : 80 = 65 : 100

(6) 2 : 3 = 4 : 6 = 6 : 9 = 8 : 12 = 10 : 15

(7) 13 : 17 = 26 : 34 = 39 : 51 = 52 : 68 = 65 : 85

(8) 13 : 21 = 26 : 42 = 39 : 63 = 52 : 84 = 65 : 105

EXERCISE NO. 13

(1) 13 : 14 = [26] : 28 = 39 : [42] = 52 : [56] = 65 : [70]

(2) 1 : 3 = [2] : 6 = 3 : [9] = 4 : [12] = 5 : [15]

(3) 13 : 17 = 26 : [34] = 39 : [51] = [52] : 68 = [65] : 85

(4) 13 : 23 = [26] : 46 = 39 : [69] = 52 : [92] = [65] : 115

(5) 2 : 3 = 4 : [6] = [6] : 9 = [8] : 12 = 10 : [15]

(6) 13 : 21 = 26 : [42] = [39] : 63 = 52 : [84] = [65] : 105

(7) 1 : 2 = 2 : [4] = [3] : 6 = [4] : 8 = 5 : [10]

(8) 1 : 4 = 2 : [8] = [3] : 12 = 4 : [16] = [5] : 20

EXERCISE NO. 14

(1) 2 : 5 = [4] : 10 = 6 : [15] = [8] : 20 = 10 : [25]

(2) 2 : 3 = 4 : [6] = 6 : [9] = 8 : [12] = 10 : [15]

(3) 9 : 11 = [18] : 22 = 27 : [33] = [36] : 44 = [45] : 55

(4) 6 : 11 = [12] : 22 = [18] : 33 = [24] : 44 = [30] : 55

(5) 9 : 22 = [18] : 44 = 27 : [66] = 36 : [88] = [45] : 110

(6) 9 : 25 = 18 : [50] = [27] : 75 = [36] : 100 = [45] : 125

(7) 6 : 7 = 12 : [14] = 18 : [21] = 24 : [28] = 30 : [35]

(8) 3 : 8 = 6 : [16] = 9 : [24] = 12 : [32] = 15 : [40]

EXERCISE NO. 15

(1) 3 : 13 = 6 : [26] = 9 : [39] = 12 : [52] = 15 : [65]

(2) 1 : 2 = 2 : [4] = 3 : [6] = 4 : [8] = 5 : [10]

(3) 3 : 7 = 6 : [14] = [9] : 21 = 12 : [28] = 15 : [35]

(4) 3 : 5 = [6] : 10 = [9] : 15 = 12 : [20] = 15 : [25]

(5) 3 : 4 = 6 : [8] = 9 : [12] = 12 : [16] = [15] : 20

(6) 3 : 10 = 6 : [20] = [9] : 30 = [12] : 40 = 15 : [50]

(7) 3 : 11 = [6] : 22 = 9 : [33] = [12] : 44 = 15 : [55]

(8) 3 : 8 = [6] : 16 = [9] : 24 = [12] : 32 = 15 : [40]

EXERCISE NO. 16

(1) 5 : 18 = [10] : 36 = 15 : [54] = [20] : 72 = [25] : 90

(2) 5 : 12 = [10] : 24 = [15] : 36 = [20] : 48 = [25] : 60

(3) 2 : 7 = 4 : [14] = 6 : [21] = 8 : [28] = [10] : 35

(4) 5 : 8 = [10] : 16 = 15 : [24] = 20 : [32] = [25] : 40

(5) 1 : 4 = [2] : 8 = [3] : 12 = 4 : [16] = 5 : [20]

(6) 5 : 9 = 10 : [18] = 15 : [27] = 20 : [36] = 25 : [45]

(7) 5 : 17 = 10 : [34] = 15 : [51] = 20 : [68] = 25 : [85]

(8) 1 : 3 = [2] : 6 = 3 : [9] = [4] : 12 = 5 : [15]

EXERCISE NO. 17

(1) $13 : 19 = \boxed{26} : 38 = 39 : \boxed{57} = \boxed{52} : 76 = \boxed{65} : 95$

(2) $13 : 20 = \boxed{26} : 40 = 39 : \boxed{60} = 52 : \boxed{80} = 65 : \boxed{100}$

(3) $13 : 14 = 26 : \boxed{28} = 39 : \boxed{42} = \boxed{52} : 56 = \boxed{65} : 70$

(4) $13 : 17 = \boxed{26} : 34 = \boxed{39} : 51 = \boxed{52} : 68 = 65 : \boxed{85}$

(5) $2 : 3 = \boxed{4} : 6 = \boxed{6} : 9 = \boxed{8} : 12 = 10 : \boxed{15}$

(6) $13 : 15 = 26 : \boxed{30} = \boxed{39} : 45 = 52 : \boxed{60} = 65 : \boxed{75}$

(7) $13 : 16 = 26 : \boxed{32} = \boxed{39} : 48 = \boxed{52} : 64 = \boxed{65} : 80$

(8) $1 : 2 = \boxed{2} : 4 = \boxed{3} : 6 = \boxed{4} : 8 = \boxed{5} : 10$

EXERCISE NO. 18

(1) $11 : 15 = 22 : \boxed{30} = \boxed{33} : 45 = \boxed{44} : 60 = \boxed{55} : 75$

(2) $5 : 11 = \boxed{10} : 22 = \boxed{15} : 33 = 20 : \boxed{44} = 25 : \boxed{55}$

(3) $11 : 14 = \boxed{22} : 28 = \boxed{33} : 42 = \boxed{44} : 56 = 55 : \boxed{70}$

(4) $5 : 6 = \boxed{10} : 12 = 15 : \boxed{18} = \boxed{20} : 24 = 25 : \boxed{30}$

(5) $11 : 12 = \boxed{22} : 24 = \boxed{33} : 36 = \boxed{44} : 48 = 55 : \boxed{60}$

(6) $5 : 13 = 10 : \boxed{26} = \boxed{15} : 39 = 20 : \boxed{52} = 25 : \boxed{65}$

(7) $11 : 13 = 22 : \boxed{26} = \boxed{33} : 39 = \boxed{44} : 52 = \boxed{55} : 65$

(8) $1 : 2 = 2 : \boxed{4} = \boxed{3} : 6 = \boxed{4} : 8 = 5 : \boxed{10}$

EXERCISE NO. 19

(1) $2 : 3 = 4 : \boxed{6} = 6 : \boxed{9} = \boxed{8} : 12 = 10 : \boxed{15}$

(2) $1 : 2 = \boxed{2} : 4 = 3 : \boxed{6} = 4 : \boxed{8} = 5 : \boxed{10}$

(3) $5 : 11 = \boxed{10} : 22 = \boxed{15} : 33 = \boxed{20} : 44 = \boxed{25} : 55$

(4) $5 : 6 = 10 : \boxed{12} = \boxed{15} : 18 = \boxed{20} : 24 = \boxed{25} : 30$

(5) $5 : 12 = 10 : \boxed{24} = \boxed{15} : 36 = \boxed{20} : 48 = 25 : \boxed{60}$

(6) $5 : 13 = 10 : \boxed{26} = \boxed{15} : 39 = 20 : \boxed{52} = 25 : \boxed{65}$

(7) $2 : 5 = 4 : \boxed{10} = 6 : \boxed{15} = 8 : \boxed{20} = 10 : \boxed{25}$

(8) $5 : 8 = 10 : \boxed{16} = 15 : \boxed{24} = 20 : \boxed{32} = 25 : \boxed{40}$

EXERCISE NO. 20

(1) $15 : 16 = \boxed{30} : 32 = 45 : \boxed{48} = 60 : \boxed{64} = 75 : \boxed{80}$

(2) $9 : 10 = 18 : \boxed{20} = 27 : \boxed{30} = \boxed{36} : 40 = 45 : \boxed{50}$

(3) $13 : 17 = \boxed{26} : 34 = \boxed{39} : 51 = \boxed{52} : 68 = \boxed{65} : 85$

(4) $5 : 6 = \boxed{10} : 12 = \boxed{15} : 18 = 20 : \boxed{24} = 25 : \boxed{30}$

(5) $9 : 11 = 18 : \boxed{22} = 27 : \boxed{33} = \boxed{36} : 44 = 45 : \boxed{55}$

(6) $15 : 19 = \boxed{30} : 38 = 45 : \boxed{57} = 60 : \boxed{76} = \boxed{75} : 95$

(7) $3 : 4 = \boxed{6} : 8 = 9 : \boxed{12} = 12 : \boxed{16} = 15 : \boxed{20}$

(8) $15 : 17 = \boxed{30} : 34 = \boxed{45} : 51 = \boxed{60} : 68 = 75 : \boxed{85}$

EXERCISE NO. 21

1) Which two teachers received equivalent ratios of apples from their total number of students? Brown and Hearn

Teachers	Received Apples	Number of Students
Brown	2	34
Hearn	3	51
Theodore	2	36
Jones	3	48

2) Which two types of cars have equivalent ratios of miles traveled to gallons of gas used? Toyota and Dodge

Cars	Miles Traveled	Gallons of Gas Used
Chevrolet	27	3
Toyota	64	4
Ford	25	2
Dodge	48	3

3) Which two recipes have equivalent ratios of cups of flour needed to the number of cookies? Sugar and Macadamia Nut

Recipes	Cups of Flour Needed	Number of Cookies
Sugar	4	32
Macadamia Nut	5	40
Chocolate Chip	4	34
Peanut Butter	2	17

EXERCISE NO. 22

1) Which two baseball games have equivalent ratios of walks to the number of runs scored? Yankees and Cubs

Games	Walks	Number of Runs Scored
Yankees	2	17
Braves	5	40
Red Sox	4	32
Cubs	4	34

2) Which two types of cars have equivalent ratios of miles traveled to gallons of gas used? Ford and Lexus

Cars	Miles Traveled	Gallons of Gas Used
Fiat	46	3
Ford	42	3
Toyota	48	4
Lexus	28	2

3) Which two recycling plants have equivalent ratios of green bottles to the total number of bottles recycled in one day? Plant A and Plant D

Recycling Plants	Green Bottles Recycled	Total Bottles Recycled
Plant A	23	115
Plant B	48	216
Plant C	50	260
Plant D	64	320

EXERCISE NO. 23

1) Which two types of cars have equivalent ratios of miles traveled to gallons of gas used? Chevrolet and Fiat

Cars	Miles Traveled	Gallons of Gas Used
Chevrolet	22	2
Toyota	40	4
Fiat	33	3
Ford	32	3

2) Which two recycling plants have equivalent ratios of green bottles to the total number of bottles recycled in one day? Plant A and Plant C

Recycling Plants	Green Bottles Recycled	Total Bottles Recycled
Plant A	13	104
Plant B	18	140
Plant C	32	256
Plant D	24	196

3) Which two city parks have equivalent ratios of planted maple trees to the total number of trees in the park? Eastern and Central

City Parks	Maple Trees Planted	Total Trees Planted
South Side	24	158
Eastern	42	294
Central	17	119
North Ridge	36	248

EXERCISE NO. 24

1) Which two types of cars have equivalent ratios of miles traveled to hours of time during the trip? Chevrolet and Toyota

Cars	Miles Traveled	Hours of Time
Chevrolet	34	2
Toyota	51	3
Lexus	36	2
Honda	48	3

2) Which two teachers received equivalent ratios of apples from their total number of students? Theodore and Brown

Teachers	Received Apples	Number of Students
Jones	3	46
Theodore	3	42
Brown	2	28
Smith	4	48

3) Which two recipes have equivalent ratios of cups of flour needed to the number of cookies? Chocolate Chip and Peanut Butter

Recipes	Cups of Flour Needed	Number of Cookies
Chocolate Chip	3	48
Macadamia Nut	2	25
Peanut Butter	4	64
Oatmeal Raisin	3	27

EXERCISE NO. 25

1) Which two recipes have equivalent ratios of cups of flour needed to the number of cookies? Oatmeal Raisin and Macadamia Nut

Recipes	Cups of Flour Needed	Number of Cookies
Oatmeal Raisin	2	17
Sugar	4	32
Macadamia Nut	4	34
Peanut Butter	5	40

2) Which two types of cars have equivalent ratios of miles traveled to gallons of gas used? Ford and Fiat

Cars	Miles Traveled	Gallons of Gas Used
Toyota	25	2
Ford	64	4
Fiat	48	3
Dodge	27	3

3) Which two baseball games have equivalent ratios of walks to the number of runs scored? Marlins and Red Sox

Games	Walks	Number of Runs Scored
Braves	1	14
Yankees	2	32
Marlins	2	24
Red Sox	3	36

EXERCISE NO. 26

1) 2 red bikes out of 24 bikes $\frac{1}{12}$

2) 5 inches to 25 inches $\frac{1}{5}$

3) 32 footballs to 48 footballs $\frac{2}{3}$

4) 8 snow days out of 332 days $\frac{2}{83}$

5) 6 blue cars out of 21 cars $\frac{2}{7}$

6) 12 points out of 24 points $\frac{1}{2}$

7) 6 feet out of 42 feet $\frac{1}{7}$

8) 6 cups to 48 cups $\frac{1}{8}$

9) 18 gallons to 33 gallons $\frac{6}{11}$

10) 40 pounds to 50 pounds $\frac{4}{5}$

11) 8 beetles out of 20 insects $\frac{2}{5}$

12) 14 pints to 21 pints $\frac{2}{3}$

13) 33 miles out of 36 miles $\frac{11}{12}$

14) 4 quarts to 12 quarts $\frac{1}{3}$

15) 7 nickels to 70 nickels $\frac{1}{10}$

16) 49 rainy days out of 56 days $\frac{7}{8}$

17) 8 dimes out of 20 coins $\frac{2}{5}$

18) 28 dimes to 49 dimes $\frac{4}{7}$

EXERCISE NO. 27

1) 28 points out of 40 points $\frac{7}{10}$

2) 15 footballs to 18 footballs $\frac{5}{6}$

3) 5 nickels to 25 nickels $\frac{1}{5}$

4) 12 dimes to 72 dimes $\frac{1}{6}$

5) 20 snow days out of 45 days $\frac{4}{9}$

6) 7 pounds to 28 pounds $\frac{1}{4}$

7) 4 dimes out of 14 coins $\frac{2}{7}$

8) 20 feet out of 48 feet $\frac{5}{12}$

9) 40 beetles out of 55 insects $\frac{8}{11}$

10) 12 cups to 21 cups $\frac{4}{7}$

11) 10 cakes out of 18 cakes $\frac{5}{9}$

12) 18 miles out of 36 miles $\frac{1}{2}$

13) 7 inches to 49 inches $\frac{1}{7}$

14) 22 quarts to 24 quarts $\frac{11}{12}$

15) 2 pennies to 24 pennies $\frac{1}{12}$

16) 24 rainy days out of 48 days $\frac{1}{2}$

17) 12 pints to 66 pints $\frac{2}{11}$

18) 42 red bikes out of 49 bikes $\frac{6}{7}$

EXERCISE NO. 28

1) 10 pennies to 35 pennies $\frac{2}{7}$

2) 24 inches to 27 inches $\frac{8}{9}$

3) 24 cups to 40 cups $\frac{3}{5}$

4) 12 red bikes out of 30 bikes $\frac{2}{5}$

5) 48 quarts to 60 quarts $\frac{4}{5}$

6) 35 miles out of 55 miles $\frac{7}{11}$

7) 42 snow days out of 54 days $\frac{7}{9}$

8) 14 blue cars out of 84 cars $\frac{1}{6}$

9) 15 rainy days out of 33 days $\frac{5}{11}$

10) 2 dimes out of 6 coins $\frac{1}{3}$

11) 4 feet out of 6 feet $\frac{2}{3}$

12) 30 nickels to 55 nickels $\frac{6}{11}$

13) 20 gallons to 25 gallons $\frac{4}{5}$

14) 42 points out of 56 points $\frac{3}{4}$

15) 4 pounds to 44 pounds $\frac{1}{11}$

16) 12 beetles out of 14 insects $\frac{6}{7}$

17) 9 footballs to 30 footballs $\frac{3}{10}$

18) 36 cakes out of 54 cakes $\frac{2}{3}$

EXERCISE NO. 29

1) 10 gallons to 50 gallons $\frac{1}{5}$

2) 25 cups to 45 cups $\frac{5}{9}$

3) 8 footballs to 48 footballs $\frac{1}{6}$

4) 48 dimes to 66 dimes $\frac{8}{11}$

5) 9 beetles out of 30 insects $\frac{3}{10}$

6) 14 miles out of 77 miles $\frac{2}{11}$

7) 30 snow days out of 72 days $\frac{5}{12}$

8) 12 feet out of 48 feet $\frac{1}{4}$

9) 6 rainy days out of 72 days $\frac{1}{12}$

10) 25 quarts to 55 quarts $\frac{5}{11}$

11) 7 pints to 77 pints $\frac{1}{11}$

12) 24 pounds to 30 pounds $\frac{4}{5}$

13) 20 nickels to 24 nickels $\frac{5}{6}$

14) 6 pennies to 249 pennies $\frac{2}{83}$

15) 10 inches to 14 inches $\frac{5}{7}$

16) 30 points out of 48 points $\frac{5}{8}$

17) 35 cakes out of 42 cakes $\frac{5}{6}$

18) 30 blue cars out of 35 cars $\frac{6}{7}$

EXERCISE NO. 30

1) 12 feet out of 24 feet $\frac{1}{2}$

2) 12 dimes to 40 dimes $\frac{3}{10}$

3) 8 gallons to 16 gallons $\frac{1}{2}$

4) 49 quarts to 63 quarts $\frac{7}{9}$

5) 3 cakes out of 21 cakes $\frac{1}{7}$

6) 18 nickels to 20 nickels $\frac{9}{10}$

7) 48 inches to 66 inches $\frac{8}{11}$

8) 6 blue cars out of 24 cars $\frac{1}{4}$

9) 35 miles out of 56 miles $\frac{5}{8}$

10) 20 snow days out of 35 days $\frac{4}{7}$

11) 66 pints to 72 pints $\frac{11}{12}$

12) 49 rainy days out of 56 days $\frac{7}{8}$

13) 20 points out of 45 points $\frac{4}{9}$

14) 56 pounds to 70 pounds $\frac{4}{5}$

15) 6 footballs to 27 footballs $\frac{2}{9}$

16) 12 red bikes out of 28 bikes $\frac{3}{7}$

17) 14 pennies to 77 pennies $\frac{2}{11}$

18) 20 cups to 55 cups $\frac{4}{11}$

EXERCISE NO. 31

(1) $x = \frac{88 \times 93}{3} = 2728$

(6) $x = \frac{69 \times 40}{20} = 138$

(2) $x = \frac{24 \times 100}{25} = 96$

(7) $x = \frac{49 \times 18}{6} = 147$

(3) $x = \frac{73 \times 84}{4} = 1533$

(8) $x = \frac{28 \times 45}{9} = 140$

(4) $x = \frac{16 \times 15}{3} = 80$

(9) $x = \frac{7 \times 68}{17} = 28$

(5) $x = \frac{9 \times 80}{20} = 36$

(10) $x = \frac{40 \times 68}{17} = 160$

EXERCISE NO. 32

(1) $x = \frac{59 \times 52}{4} = 767$

(6) $x = \frac{15 \times 28}{7} = 60$

(2) $x = \frac{67 \times 75}{15} = 335$

(7) $x = \frac{65 \times 14}{7} = 130$

(3) $x = \frac{51 \times 66}{2} = 1683$

(8) $x = \frac{97 \times 22}{11} = 194$

(4) $x = \frac{13 \times 36}{6} = 78$

(9) $x = \frac{67 \times 96}{24} = 268$

(5) $x = \frac{74 \times 9}{3} = 222$

(10) $x = \frac{50 \times 91}{13} = 350$

EXERCISE NO. 33

(1) $x = \frac{53 \times 45}{15} = 159$

(2) $x = \frac{65 \times 51}{17} = 195$

(3) $x = \frac{3 \times 16}{2} = 24$

(4) $x = \frac{69 \times 44}{11} = 276$

(5) $x = \frac{47 \times 70}{5} = 658$

(6) $x = \frac{67 \times 45}{3} = 1005$

(7) $x = \frac{13 \times 36}{9} = 52$

(8) $x = \frac{23 \times 49}{7} = 161$

(9) $x = \frac{47 \times 14}{7} = 94$

(10) $x = \frac{57 \times 68}{4} = 969$

EXERCISE NO. 34

(1) $x = \frac{65 \times 60}{12} = 325$

(2) $x = \frac{73 \times 88}{44} = 146$

(3) $x = \frac{87 \times 46}{23} = 174$

(4) $x = \frac{72 \times 10}{5} = 144$

(5) $x = \frac{56 \times 81}{27} = 168$

(6) $x = \frac{100 \times 52}{13} = 400$

(7) $x = \frac{15 \times 74}{37} = 30$

(8) $x = \frac{67 \times 24}{12} = 134$

(9) $x = \frac{15 \times 36}{2} = 270$

(10) $x = \frac{85 \times 90}{6} = 1275$

EXERCISE NO. 35

(1) $x = \frac{53 \times 95}{19} = 265$

(2) $x = \frac{93 \times 60}{4} = 1395$

(3) $x = \frac{88 \times 21}{7} = 264$

(4) $x = \frac{69 \times 68}{34} = 138$

(5) $x = \frac{79 \times 98}{14} = 553$

(6) $x = \frac{23 \times 24}{6} = 92$

(7) $x = \frac{5 \times 81}{27} = 15$

(8) $x = \frac{63 \times 36}{2} = 1134$

(9) $x = \frac{13 \times 39}{3} = 169$

(10) $x = \frac{88 \times 38}{19} = 176$

EXERCISE NO. 36

(1) $x = \dfrac{11 \times 58}{29} = 22$ (6) $x = \dfrac{29 \times 80}{2} = 1160$

(2) $x = \dfrac{65 \times 33}{11} = 195$ (7) $x = \dfrac{31 \times 54}{9} = 186$

(3) $x = \dfrac{26 \times 49}{7} = 182$ (8) $x = \dfrac{24 \times 44}{11} = 96$

(4) $x = \dfrac{81 \times 32}{16} = 162$ (9) $x = \dfrac{6 \times 77}{11} = 42$

(5) $x = \dfrac{92 \times 35}{5} = 644$ (10) $x = \dfrac{55 \times 86}{2} = 2365$

EXERCISE NO. 37

(1) $x = \dfrac{46 \times 30}{3} = 460$ (6) $x = \dfrac{95 \times 32}{2} = 1520$

(2) $x = \dfrac{20 \times 56}{7} = 160$ (7) $x = \dfrac{93 \times 44}{11} = 372$

(3) $x = \dfrac{35 \times 78}{2} = 1365$ (8) $x = \dfrac{27 \times 8}{2} = 108$

(4) $x = \dfrac{97 \times 35}{7} = 485$ (9) $x = \dfrac{71 \times 66}{11} = 426$

(5) $x = \dfrac{67 \times 95}{19} = 335$ (10) $x = \dfrac{71 \times 18}{2} = 639$

EXERCISE NO. 38

(1) $x = \dfrac{26 \times 42}{3} = 364$ (6) $x = \dfrac{3 \times 16}{4} = 12$

(2) $x = \dfrac{3 \times 80}{5} = 48$ (7) $x = \dfrac{83 \times 72}{4} = 1494$

(3) $x = \dfrac{19 \times 99}{11} = 171$ (8) $x = \dfrac{16 \times 62}{31} = 32$

(4) $x = \dfrac{88 \times 39}{3} = 1144$ (9) $x = \dfrac{7 \times 16}{4} = 28$

(5) $x = \dfrac{59 \times 18}{6} = 177$ (10) $x = \dfrac{34 \times 69}{23} = 102$

EXERCISE NO. 39

(1) $x = \frac{14 \times 68}{17} = 56$

(2) $x = \frac{34 \times 92}{23} = 136$

(3) $x = \frac{87 \times 68}{4} = 1479$

(4) $x = \frac{46 \times 51}{3} = 782$

(5) $x = \frac{20 \times 63}{7} = 180$

(6) $x = \frac{59 \times 96}{3} = 1888$

(7) $x = \frac{51 \times 60}{10} = 306$

(8) $x = \frac{47 \times 40}{2} = 940$

(9) $x = \frac{9 \times 48}{4} = 108$

(10) $x = \frac{85 \times 56}{28} = 170$

EXERCISE NO. 40

(1) $x = \frac{19 \times 48}{3} = 304$

(2) $x = \frac{74 \times 38}{19} = 148$

(3) $x = \frac{9 \times 70}{2} = 315$

(4) $x = \frac{11 \times 84}{42} = 22$

(5) $x = \frac{57 \times 30}{10} = 171$

(6) $x = \frac{27 \times 84}{14} = 162$

(7) $x = \frac{19 \times 75}{25} = 57$

(8) $x = \frac{76 \times 57}{3} = 1444$

(9) $x = \frac{74 \times 95}{5} = 1406$

(10) $x = \frac{90 \times 63}{7} = 810$

Visit

BABY PROFESSOR
EDUCATION KIDS

www.BabyProfessorBooks.com
to download Free Baby Professor eBooks
and view our catalog of new and exciting
Children's Books

CPSIA information can be obtained
at www.ICGtesting.com
Printed in the USA
LVHW051544161222
735289LV00008B/1381